# The White Whale

J.M. Bandy

This book is dedicated to myself. I overcame a lot just to type this up. And to all the girls and women who are told they are not good enough. You are more than good enough.

# Preface

I sit writing this at a time where every day I am getting closer and closer to the completion of this book. It is surreal to me, the reality of this dream and how it started to come together on its own. I write to help me process and cope with the events and trauma in my life. Without realizing it I followed this and continued to see it through. Years of notes and writings compiled to allow me a chance to process and feel my emotions. It is a beautiful coincidence that it led to me writing this; introducing you to my world. I have always been an open book as a person. You ask, I will answer in truth but there has always been this pain. This darkness. That I have held onto and kept locked within myself. Ashamed of my shortcomings and my true emotions as I journeyed through life.

I needed an outlet that even my art would not fully provide me. I turned to writing.

If I told you this was poetic irony that would be an understatement. I do not consider myself dumb or below average however one love of mine has also been my demise. I write this while knowing my whole life I have struggled to read. Do not get me wrong. I love reading but I have never been a strong reader. If reading was a survival skill I would have died out with the dinosaurs.

Even though I have struggled, I devoured books growing up. In these fantastical worlds and adventures, I found peace. I found empathy and emotions. I cried with and fought alongside a vast collection of characters. Walking, running and flying over miles of creatively designed worlds.

Then I found poetry. I understood it instantly. The words of each poem slowly burned into my mind. From authors like Edgar Allen Poe, Charles Bukowski, Dolores Dahl and Lang Leav. They taught me the truths in life through their words. They taught how to write and how to express myself in every ink-stained page I threw myself into. I found myself somewhere tucked

in-between each line of every stanza.
This time I took care of myself. I
nurtured my inner child, once I found
her. I am gentle with her now. More so
than I have ever been. I am proud of
her and all the adversity she has
overcome.

Poetry gave me love and health. I
hope, whoever and wherever you are
reading this you find yourself among
these pages. The only request I have;
when you find **you,** be gentle and be
kind. I thank you for taking the time
to go through this journey and I hope
my words can offer at least one soul a
safe place and understanding.

"The most important things are the hardest to say. They are the things you get ashamed of because words diminish your feelings—words shrink things that seem timeless when they are in your head to no more than living size when they are brought out."

-Stephen King

# I Swear

I swear it was love

I kept you a secret

I was so young

Then I tried to speak it

You told me no

Love is not what I feel

But you kept holding tight

An unspoken promise this is real

This dance played out for many years

Holding on to the promise of you

Losing you out grew all fears

I swear it was true

So alone I grew

Without the love I swear I knew

Still holding on to the promise of you

I now swear this love was not true

# Summer Love

Summer love is not so sweet

It is not like the movies

It rips your heart out

Leaving you bleeding


It is the sourest apple

While you die of thirst

It is all that much harder

When he was your first


Sweetest strawberries are the bait

To lure you in

Distract until it is too late

That is when the loss infects you within


Summer love now tastes of grave soil

With hints of cremated ashes

The slightest reminder makes me recoil

It feels like 90 lashes

Summer love was lost too soon

The time feels like a lie

But, he is among the angels

At home above the sky.

# Mania

I always get overly excited

For a day or two

I have even been excited

For the sky being blue

I will talk endlessly

About my future too


I will prep and plan

With lavish ideals

Decorating my future

For all it appeals

Shiny and bright making this real


And then the darkness hits

I forget the dreams

I stop and quit

Imploding into myself

Like a dying star no longer lit

The dreams will wither

A flower without water

But then I come across another

Dream I start to see

The light slowly starts again

Shining bright inside of me.

# I Am

I know you probably think

I AM because of you

But I tried my whole life

To be only true

I was me before you

I stayed me

Even when you were through

And now you cannot see

I have only blossomed

And then I bloom

Never because of you

Your presence did not loom

# Freed

I write out of anger
I write out of greed
I create out of hunger
I create just to feed

This beast inside me
Gnashes and claws
Just to create beauty
Others can see

But my pen is not mightier
And my sword is still weak
So, this beast inside me
Has broken out free

# Patience

I have never been plucked.

A curse I thought

Until I saw

How I outgrew

Those who are dying

From being plucked

Too soon.

# Twin Flame

Time stands still

Our hands a blaze

My heart only beats for you

Each and every day

# The Universe

The secret to the universe

Is something I have yet to know

But curiosity gets to me

With her ever-inquiring flow

I have dreamt about it often

That once my heart has met its match

The secrets they would soften

At our fingertips they latch

And so, my heart will sing

A song for you to hear

And when it rings aloud

It means that we are near

# Uniquely

I wanted to be just like you

I wanted to be an outcast

I wanted to be so unique

I wanted to fit in

Just sitting by waiting

For real life to begin

# Effortless Smile

We all want to be unique

In our own way

We want to be insightful

Deep. We want our problems to resonate

Through the collective

We want that one person

To fall in love with us undoubtedly

Because they see our uniqueness

We all want to be the pixie dream girl

Dancing fluttering through life unashamed

Uninhibited.

We want our lives to be filled with the
dream haze

To be the Cinderella of our story

Because we are unique, and no one is like
us.

No one is as passionate

No one is as loving

No one is as accepting

Reality is far too painful.

So, we force ourselves into this false
idea of perfection.

But truth is we are not unique

Not in our kindness

Not in our style

Not in the way I have perfected my
crooked "effortless" smile.

# The White Whale

I have touched the white whale

I have felt his breath upon my neck

Whispering to me in a foreign tongue

The cold touch of skin to skin

With our bodies entwined

We became one, one heart beating

For two minds

It filled me to the bitter edge

Loving me for what I truly was

Do you think happiness?

It is not so simple

Heavily relying on another to keep me
afloat

I collapsed.

He tore himself from my body

Leaving behind broken bones

Arteries bleeding out

And so, I sank

Unable to breathe

Water filled my lungs

My vision blurred

I was gone.

Lost to the uncharted depths alone.

# Driving Me Mad

I wanted to tell you how I feel

I wanted to tell you so bad

I want to scream and yell it

At the top of my lungs

Because it is driving me mad

# Beast and Man

Blood pours from his mouth

Confused he wakes miles south

He felt the beast start to retreat

As the taste goes sour from sweet

The wild inside is tamed for now

30 more days and he must allow

At the full moon the beast will howl.

# Wrong

I have gazed at the empty shell and saw
inside

I have stared into the vast emptiness of
the cornea

And saw light.

You expressed to me words I took to heart

Now I struggle to show you the words have
taken flight

Once I fell apart.

I was broken and spiraled out of control

I am hurt and empty, the world has taken
its toll.

But now you are back

The same as before

And I no longer have the taste of sweet.

I am bitter and linger for too long

It is too late; I now am all wrong.

# Monthly

Paper planes

And summer haze

Reminds me of the good days

Tear stained cheek

And feeling meek

Reminds me of my worst week

Bleeding first

Living this curse

Reminds me it just got worse

Losing breath

Missing flesh

Reminds me of my tragic death.

# Harvester

It was alone

Peaceful

Living naturally

Like it should

You came along without thought or care

You plucked it from its home

You ignored what it needed

And cared only to steal its beauty.

Surely something so beautiful

Needed to be owned

To be caged

And taken from it's home

When it withered

Decay and dying

You did not mourn for the life you took

You tossed it aside disgusted

The beauty you once held

Was gone

You wanted nothing from it

It was disposable

Gone and then forgotten

And you continue

To trample

And pick the next beauty

That catches your eye.

# Do You See Me?

You do not see me.

I want you to see me

The light inside the dark

The soul inside this shell

I want you to see my spark.

# Life Cycle

I hear them breathing

Singing to the moon

I hear them crying

Screaming in agony

But I see them dancing

Swirling around in the purest form

Silence.

There is silence.

Dried and rotting

Cut from their very source of life

Treated as if they are nothing

But you do not hear it like I do

The screams of betrayal

The cries of pain

Burning alive

Dismembered.

And then I hear it

I hear them breathing

# The Sea and The Moon

I've got the full moon in my back pocket
You ask if you can see
Do not steal a look
I've got nothing much with me

Sea, he has the ocean
In the palm of his hand
He said he has been trying for years
Just to find some land

This is my little secret
No one is allowed to know
You ask me if one day
I will decide to show

No, but if you steal it
I might give you a chance
Because one day it is destined
The moon will teach the sea to dance

And as destiny goes

The sea follows the moon

And only she knows

Why does the sea swoon?

# Do you ever?

Bite your nails until they bleed
Lie to a love you will never see
Say the truth straight to me?

Dance naked in the dark
Make art without a mark
Hear me speak without my snark?

Taste something perfectly sweet
Stand in a puddle with bare feet
Enjoy our time when we meet?

# Your Pillar

I will be your pillar

To help you stand tall

I will be your sword

As you defend them all

I will be your guide

To lead you when you are lost

I will be there to pay

So you never know the cost

I will be by your side

When you are all alone

I will be your star

To guide you back home

I will show you love

To shield you from the hate

I have seen your soul

I know this is our fate.

# Vows

Skin to skin

Flesh to flesh

Time to take the final test


I take you until my death

Do you take me with your last breath?

# Selfish

I ask that when I leave
You try to remember me
I want a song to come on
That will make you see

I want you to hear
My whispered breath
Dancing in your ear
Proving that I am still here

I want you to feel my hair
Draped along your arm
When you look, I am not there
Still trapped by my charm

I want you to see my blood
From every wound you cause
Vision filled with red
Was this my only flaw?

I will haunt you, eternally

Nightmares filled with my screams

You will think this devilish

Because I decided to be selfish

# Butterflies

The soft flutter
Grazing the inside
My nerves on fire
Burning alive

You walked in
My breath escaped
You made it feel
Like a summer's day

I stole your attention
But all eyes stayed on you
When you kissed me
I could not move

I am flush with anticipation
My face burns
It is a conflagration
My heart yearns

Quickly I will shut you down

For my own diluted security

Even if I want it to surround

Like a chrysalis caging me

# Past Life

I have seen you before

Not in this place

I have felt you before

Not with this face.

I have hugged you before

Heart to heart

They danced when they met

And cried when they part

We have fought here before

For a different crime

I have loved you before

In a different time

I have touched you before

Hand to hand

A blanket of peace

A connection so grand.

# The Hole

The day you climbed in my bed
You burned a spot
Inside my head

And now your side is bare
Sheets still twisted
From when you were here

And the bed has gotten so cold
I am haunted by
Our plans to grow old.

My pillow stained with all the tears
The pain manifests
A hole in my chest appears.

# A Misunderstanding

I am comfortable in my anger
And my emptiness
I find comfort in my tears
And all the loneliness

I expect you all to leave
At some time very soon
Forever is so hard to believe
It feels like chasing the moon.

It almost seems impossible
To keep a friendship around
Yours is just another one
I will bury in the ground

So tonight, I am wishing you adieu
You seem to have moved on
Do not let your last words be
'You have gotten this all wrong'

Because every time I hear those words

A shiver goes down my spine

It is burned inside my memory

I hear it all the time.

# I Feel

I feel I have a lot to say.

A lot of questions posed at the universe.


I feel I have a lot to see.

A lot of dancing stars and the smiling
moon looking out for me.


I feel I have a lot to hear.

The trees will sing, and the flowers'
voices appear.


I feel I have a lot to feel.

Love's first kiss and hearts to steal.


I feel I have too much to say.

I struggle to find the words to convey
but I will keep talking just to say.


I feel I have too much to see.

Time will not be helpful to me, but I'll
keep looking just to see.


I feel I have too much to hear.

My mind runs wild from just my ear, but I
will keep listening just to hear.

I feel I have too much to feel.

I long for a lover that is real, but I
will keep loving just to feel.

# What You Stole

The places that you touched
Still burn uncomfortably
Reminding me of that night
You took away from me.

You stole my uniqueness
And my independence too
You stole the one thing
I swore I would never lose.

You took away my confidence
That I had within myself
To know the one person, I rely on
Was always just myself.

Now I cannot even rely on
The oneself I will never rid
You showed me I'm a coward
My self-worth you undid.

It hurt to watch me let down

My inner child that depended

On my strength to be found

And now that child ended.

# Dear God

Dear God,

I used to pray when I was young to keep away the evil that lurked at night. I would pray to keep me safe and pray to keep me sane. I'd pray when I was burdened by the sorrows that I felt. I prayed for solis. I prayed for help. I prayed for the pain to go away. I prayed for love to always stay. As I grew no answers came and everything stayed the very same. My pain and sorrow are heavy in my heart. So, I prayed for a fresh start.

I begged and begged and never was saved. I cried and screamed, and you stayed away. I suddenly realized you are not the one I need to idolize. Abandoned by the one who was supposed to never leave. I stopped praying and I knew I no longer believe.

I found on the other side a person to believe in. I found someone who will never lie or leave. I found someone to rely on someone I could see.

I found my reflection and in that I found myself. I found the child that was lost and begging for help. I reached inside my open heart and took her hand in mine. I promised her I will be here and now everything will be fine.

# May 7th

To my darkest day

And my darkest hours.

I will never be the same.


I have written this a hundred times over.

Each word never doing full justice to the
person you were.

The kindness in your eyes hid the pain
the world was so blind to.


Your laugh was so infectious

Your smile was so contagious

Your heart was so capacious


I will never breathe the same

I will never see the same

I will never love the same


I felt the cord around your neck

Suffocating me.

I felt your consciousness slipping away

Blurring all that I see.

I felt your soul slide out of my hand

I felt you were set free.


This world was a burden to a soul like
yours and I do not blame you for walking
through that door.


But I will continue to mourn every second
of this day

because You stole my heart

And with you it went away.

# Fairytale

I want to write about how I was saved
How love brought me back

I want to write about the brink
Pulling me back before I could blink

I want to write about a fairytale
But I know my words would fail.

I want to write a glorious lie
So everyone will believe I am fine.

But the truth is far more interesting
I am blind and bleeding
Left on the edge to fall alone
But I hold on.

With every muscle burning
I will not let go.
I will hold on.

# The Lessons

He taught me love

He taught me laughter

He taught me my worth and beauty

He taught me how to be loved

And how to be free.

He taught me how to cry

And taught me about grief

He taught me how to cope

He taught me to believe

He taught me how to build my walls up

Right after he broke them down

Most importantly he taught me

Love did not keep him safe and sound

# Charmed Us

Everyone has said

I tend to cope so well

'You are so positive

For being dragged through hell.'


But these people have never seen

My anger and my darkness

They have never heard my true scream

They say 'You have simply charmed us.'

# Sexuality

My comfort in my sexuality

Naturally did not come

But you helped me be

The confidence I have become


I was young and ravenous

You helped me tame the beast

The world told me it was blasphemous

You let me endlessly feast


You gave me what I craved

But you were never truly mine

I was deeply depraved

And you made me feel fine


You let me gorge myself on you

Filling up my soul

Now you have moved on

Left me out in the cold

My time with you has given me

A chance to tame the beast

With you gone I now

Allow her to be released.

# Wild Woman

I am a wild woman
Free to roam this earth
I allow myself to be
Just as I am

I will speak my mind loudly
And I can be somewhat lewd
But I am a strong force
I will not change my attitude

I have been told
I am prettier when I smile
I just need to lose a few pounds
Then I will beguile

I will continue to roar with the tigers
I will run with the antelope
I will beat my chest
To show my dominance
But you will continue to detest.

# Stupid

I have been called stupid

Time and time again

I have been treated

Like I just do not understand


Your pompous attitude

Catches me off guard

I will continue my soliloquy

Just to bombard


Do you understand

When I speak in idioms

Using hypotheticals

My ego is iridium

Corrosion resistant

Atomically number 77

I am always persistent.


Do not try to embarrass me

By things you can fact check

You are more than welcome to

I will not object

I know when to admit I am wrong

And I know when I am right

Do not Insult me

Because you are just a blight

On this page

These words I will not erase

Maybe next time It will be your stage.

# Calling

When life began

The stars whispered out my name

They told me my true calling

They told me why I came


I was told of days of darkness

Trials I will face

The lonely people I will encounter

They told me I am their grace


They said these people will come along

And latch on to you fiercely

They will take all you have

And leave you, perversely.


Only once they are full

They will move on from you

Finding their meaning

The one for them that is true.


Do not be disheartened

Do not be broken down
They say I am still the one
Wearing the crown

You will hurt
So they can heal
That is your truest meaning
That is when your life will be
Fullest and teeming

You are here to heal
And love those who are stealing
Remember you are the strength
They all will be needing.

# Belief

I think I found what I believe in
Among other cultures
I think I found what I believe in
Outside of all the others

The hatred and abuse
Spewed all over our minds
I had to find something
That deeply aligned

I think I found it East
From travels I have yet to go
I think I will leave the West
For another home.

# Natural Talent

I have been complimented of my talents
My "Natural born skill"
I have been told this is a gift
I need to use it well

They do not know
The hours I have worked.
They do not see
Every one of my efforts.

Years of painstaking doubt
Mastering the essentials--
In my life this was paramount
A hobby turned crisis becoming
existential.

# Siren's Song

Nature, it calls to me

Like a siren's song

Carrying my soul to sea

My body will surely long,

To journey to my soul

Among the crashing waves

Dark and starry nights

Floating on the pirates' grave

My soul will taste of salt and sea

My eyes will only meet

At the shoreline

Letting the waves kiss my feet.

Forever longing to be at sea.

# Jellyfish

Jellies live the life
I truly wish to live
Thousands of them gather
Just to simply swim.

A creature of curiosity
No brain to be corrupt
A body protected by
Stinging tentacles erupt.

Free to live out at sea
Dancing in the waves
Peaceful, let them be
Or they leave you in a grave

Their beauty blooms
When they gather
To never be alone
I want to be a jellyfish
In the sea that is my home.

# Phony

I hate that I miss

The people who have hurt me,

The ones who never give me time

Who decided to desert me.


I hate that isolation

Has made me very lonely

Because now I want those friends

That are completely phony.

# Are you afraid?

You  told me you are not afraid of me
That is when I knew
You buried yourself inside my soul
Suddenly, without warning you withdrew.

I tried to let time heal
Then every time I saw you
The scabs I did peel
A shaky breath I drew

I tried to take everything slow
I wanted to be your friend
But you only use me when your low
This friendship is just pretend.

# For The Women

Who are loud when they laugh

Who get so nervous they cannot speak

Who command a room.

Who stand up for themselves and

For those who cannot.

This is for all the women

Who are bluntly honest

Who are not soft around the edges

Who have stretch marks and hairy thighs.

This is for all the women

Who are called "bitch" instead of boss.

Who are looked down on for being "used"
or "damaged".

This is for all the women

Who are not seen as "innocent"

Who are fierce in the face of adversity

This is for all the women

Who are independent

So independent that it is hard to imagine
any other way.

This is for all the women

Who have been forgotten

Who have been told they are better off
alone.

So they stop trying.

This is for all the women

And this is for me.

# Butterfly Effect

When you were young

You fluttered your wings

Leaving a mark

Inside my being


The flutter tickled in my soul

Filling me up

Until I was whole


I was not prepared

When the mark you left in my heart

Turned into a hurricane

Tearing me apart.

# Dark Scars

You stole my present

You stole my past

You stole my childhood

That would not last.


You stole my voice

You stole my music

You stole my soul

You abused it.


Your preyed on me

and took control

You killed me slowly

I paid the toll.


Sometimes I wonder

About a life without you

I always remember

That would not be true.


I have healed

Let go over the years

But the scars are still dark

They still bring up tears.

# To New Friends

To all my now friends
That have come this far
That have read each word
And touched each scar

Join me for a cup of coffee,
Or maybe a stiffer drink
We will talk throughout the  night
About all that you think

I will sit and listen
To all you have to say
Because you took the time
To read what is in my brain

You joined me on my journey
Through happiness and pain
You felt my same loss
You rejoiced in my gain

Now I will take the time

To listen to you too

I want to join your journey

Because that is what friends do.

107

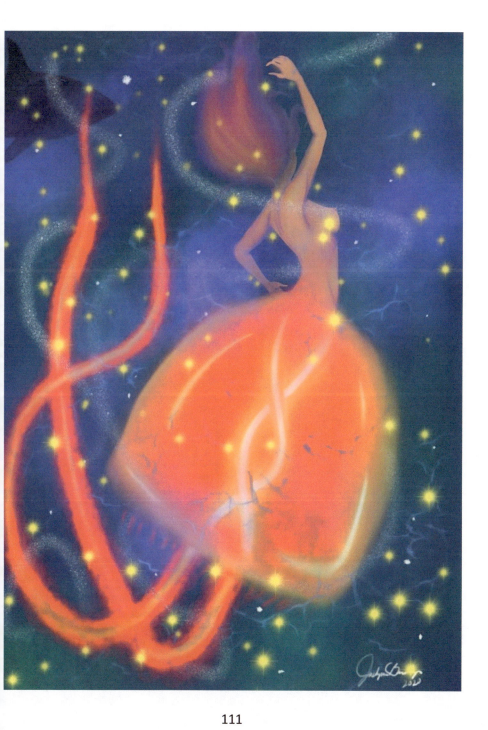

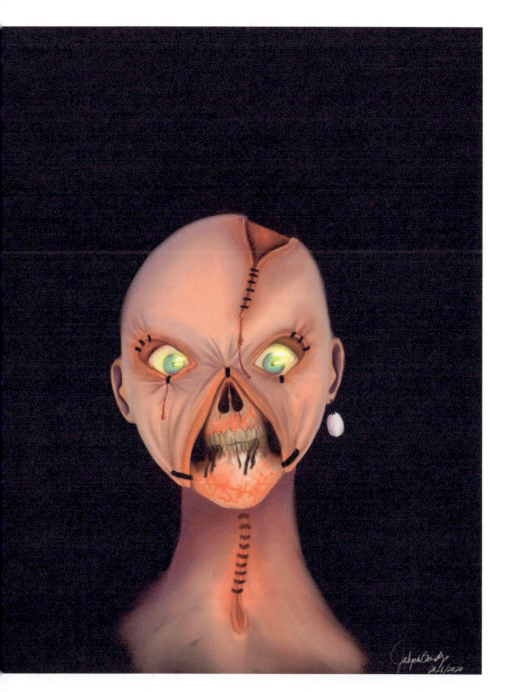

113

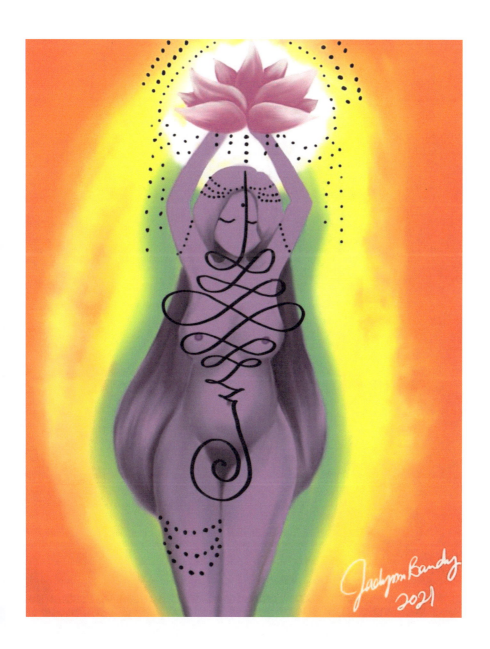

115

# About the author:

Jaclynn M. Bandy currently resides in the capital city of Salem, Oregon. Although she was also born in Salem she grew up roughly 20 miles south in the town of Albany. For the past 10 years she has lived and worked all over Oregon. Inspired by the Oregon beaches, Jaclynn loves to frequent the coast and even live in Seaside for a short while.

Jaclynn doesn't have many impressive accomplishments to speak of and barely graduated high school. She does consider herself to be an expert in having emotional breakdowns and losing keys. The most notable accomplishment of Jaclynn's was when she wrote an article in high school. This article although, poorly written and not controversial, personally offended multiple teachers. She is also very proud of the moment a teacher asked her "Are you an Idiot?" And when she failed her art classes. Yes, she hand-drew the cover art of this book. No, it does not make any sense.

Now at 27 years old, she has taken to
putting herself out there in the form of
poetry. She has a crude sense of humor,
even though not apparent in this
collection. She tends to laugh at
inappropriate times and will always make
jokes in dark situations. She is
extremely talkative and socially
outgoing. Fun fact about Jaclynn, if you
feed her, she will be your forever
friend.

Made in United States
Troutdale, OR
02/26/2024

17959654R00069